SALES & MARKETING ALIGNMENT THROUGH CONTENT

Printed in the United States of America

First Printing, 2015

ISBN-13: 978-1514228708

Printed by CreateSpace, An Amazon.com Company

www.CreateSpace.com

TABLE OF CONTENTS

FOREWORD   01

INTRODUCTION   03

CHAPTER 1: ALIGNMENT STARTS WITH CONTENT   05

CHAPTER 2: LEVERAGING YOUR SALES TEAM   11

CHAPTER 3: THE METRICS THAT DRIVE ALIGNMENT   15

CHAPTER 4: SALESPEOPLE ARE BECOMING
MINI-MARKETERS   21

CHAPTER 5: ATTENTION MARKETING: DON'T SEND
EMAILS ON BEHALF OF SALES   29

CHAPTER 6: HOW TO PULL IT ALL TOGETHER   33

SALES AND MARKETING ALIGNMENT
SUCCESS STORY: HACKERRANK   38

TOOLS FOR SALES AND MARKETING ALIGNMENT   42

SALES AND MARKETING EXPERTS   45

ABOUT TOUTAPP   48

REFERENCES   51

FOREWORD

Not too long ago I was an Inside Sales Representative at a tech company. I had a love/hate relationship with my Marketing team. I loved the people but hated what they produced. You see, they were measured by quantity and not quality, so as a sales person I was forced to sift through list after list of names and companies to find a real prospect, and don't get me started on cold calling.

So I turned to social media and became the leading thought leader of what is now called Social Selling. The world of Sales and Marketing will never be the same.

I remember the exact moment I was introduced to ToutApp at an event in San Francisco. It was 2012 and the person explaining the application to me was so passionate and clear about how this was going to revolutionize the world of email analytics, I was enchanted. Not just by the product but by the culture this company had already started in their earliest of days. As you can probably tell, I am a huge fan and supporter of ToutApp and the vision Tawheed Kader, CEO and Founder, is building. So when I was asked to contribute to this book, I was honored and excited.

This book doesn't just cover the theory of Sales and Marketing alignment, it contains actionable tips and insights from one of the leading companies in real-time email tracking and analytics. It's a guide for Sales and Marketing people to stop talking about how they can align and actually start DOING it. Enjoy.

- Koka Sexton

INTRODUCTION

Sales and Marketing are the two most crucial teams for every B2B company. A 2011 Aberdeen Group study reported that aligned organizations experienced an average of **31.6%** year-over-year growth in annual company revenue while less aligned companies experienced an average of **6.7%** growth. And yet, Sales and Marketing still tend to work in silos in most organizations.

Today, many organizations lack alignment due to one or more of the following reasons:

- Lack of communicating and exchanging goals
- Disparate vision of their ideal customer
- No insight and visibility into the other team
- Success is measured differently
- Teams work within their own set of tools and databases
- Lack of processes in place, which makes it impossible to keep track of what works

Companies often say that alignment between Sales and Marketing involves too many complex steps. Authors writing about alignment in the past have even claimed that Sales and Marketing are from two completely different planets.

This is all nonsense. We believe that the fundamental disconnect between Sales and Marketing is the fact that Marketing tends to think in terms of aggregates (buyer personas, categories, segments) while Sales tends to think in terms of distinct deals (buyer, prospects, opportunities).

In this book, we'll break down all the necessary steps, provide industry-leading expertise and present an actionable guide on everything you need to drive alignment so your organization can become one of the few that experience an average **31.6%** year-over-year growth through alignment.

CHAPTER 1: ALIGNMENT STARTS WITH CONTENT

A yearly report conducted by the Content Marketing Institute found that B2B companies are investing **28%** of their total marketing budget on content marketing, and **55%** said they'd increase their spending on it within the next 12 months. And yet, in a report by the International Data Corporation, it stated that "sales team members don't use as much as **80%** of the content that Marketing generates even though most of it was created for sales and channel enablement."

For an industry that is investing more and increasing their total budget on content marketing, the 80% statistic is rather alarming.

Even if Sales and Marketing have different priorities and personalities, it's important to note that they share a common goal of increasing revenue. Therefore, the two teams must learn to put their differences aside and drive alignment.

Sales and Marketing Alignment Starts with an Agenda

The first step in alignment is to set up a recurring meeting where stakeholders from Sales and Markeing talk. Both teams must agree upon their cadence of meetings, whether weekly or bi-weekly, and both sides must come prepared with an agenda.To drive alignment, Sales and Marketing must meet each other halfway and learn how to talk to each other in a constructive manner.

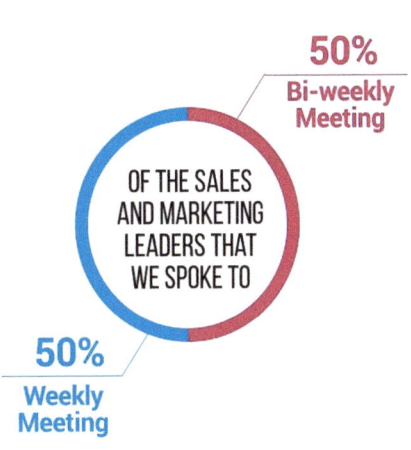

50%
Bi-weekly Meeting

OF THE SALES AND MARKETING LEADERS THAT WE SPOKE TO

50%
Weekly Meeting

Here are baseline talking points on how to alleviate difficulties in discussion, collaboration and implementation:

- Have a dedicated time where you'll compare notes on what's going on with your team, in the market and with prospects.
- Pinpoint the areas and stages within the sales process where Sales is encountering friction, confusion or competitive pressures.
- Talk through the challenges that are top of mind for your prospects that the Sales team members are coming across during their calls.

Based on the talking points above, marketers and salespeople should be able to discuss and brainstorm the following:

- Types of content that can be created to aid those friction, confusion or competitive pressures
- Types of content that Marketing can generate to help drive more qualified leads to Sales

“ There's a lot of feedback that's not represented by data or in the information that you can find in Salesforce. So, every week, the Director of Sales Development and myself sit down and have a 1:1 and strive to make sure we're aligned. He's aware of everything that's going on in Marketing, and I know the ins and outs of Sales. ”

—
Tomasz Borys
Director of Marketing, KISSmetrics

Sales and Marketing Need to Define Content Strategy Together

The Content Marketing Institute study gathered that **86%** of B2B companies use Content Marketing and **70%** of B2B marketers are creating more content than they did one year ago. Thus, once Sales and Marketing agree upon a cadence of meetings, that they follow through on the next steps.

Don't create content that will become part of the **80%** statistic; instead create content around what will aide the sales process.

Based on the discussion and results that took place in step one, the key here is for Marketing to create relevant content that can be easily deployed to the Sales team and that empowers them to use the content.

While creating content, it's the marketer's job to fulfill the Sales department's needs, it's equally important that the marketer doesn't forget to empathize with the prospect.

" When we strategize about how best to communicate value in the sales process, what we are really talking about is education. And a large part of the opportunity to succeed in sales hinges on your ability to help prospective customers clearly understand the value being offered by your product or service."

—
Thomas A. Freese
Secrets of Question Based Selling

This means that marketers and salespeople should create and share content that reflects their prospect's values.

And the only way to know your prospect's values is to have an open discussion about those values, pain points and pressures. Then, while Marketing is creating the content, Sales should constantly stay in touch with Marketing and ensure that the content created represents the voice, tonality and style that will resonate with prospects.

- Curate content that targets a specific role, industry or problem.
- Create content such as a case study, white paper or customer testimonial that addresses each step in the buyer's journey.

The way that we started aligning Sales and Marketing came down to producing thoughtful collateral that aligned with our resident goals and interests.

—
Kyle Poretto
Former Sales Development Manager, NewsCred

Organize and Test Content

As content is created, Sales and Marketing need to come together once again to walk through the created content and ensure that both sides understand how each of the items can be used as a secret weapon in the sales process.

Marketing needs to organize the created content into actionable packages that Sales can quickly find and share with prospects (more in **Chapter Six**). As Sales uses content, Marketing and Sales must have a proper system in place to test not only which content is being used, but also if the content is positively impacting the metrics that matter: revenue, conversion and overall effectiveness (more in **Chapter Three**).

Here's how you can organize your marketing content:

- Break down the buyer's journey into the different stages of the sales funnel that ensures that Sales has the right access and content.
- Test the organization system in a Sales role-play scenario where a rep sends content to a prospect.
- Give constructive feedback on the organization system and iterate on the system making it better and better.
- Spread the word: When a new piece of content is added to the system, let everyone know.

Finally, here's a four-point checklist for determining the perfect piece of content to send out to a prospect:

- ☐ Is it valuable?
- ☐ Is it clear?
- ☐ Will this change my relationship with my prospect?
- ☐ What is the ultimate call to action?

If you can check off the above points, then you've got a piece of content that's ready for your prospect's inbox.

> Sales and Marketing needs to function as one operation, and when you create that overlap, you have a very clear conversation around what's working and what's not and you're allowed to iterate much faster.

Koka Sexton
Group Manager, Content and Social Team, Corporate Communications, LinkedIn

The Key Takeaway

If a piece of content isn't being used, then it doesn't stand a chance of connecting with prospects or increasing revenue. As Sales is moving towards being more authentic and consultative, they need to work together with Marketing and provide valuable information to their prospects. In the next chapter, we'll discuss how Marketing can get visibility into their Sales teams and how to actually work together in a meaningful way.

CHAPTER 2: LEVERAGING YOUR SALES TEAM

Differences aside, Sales and Marketing both work toward a singular goal of increasing revenue. And when they learn how to get visibility into each other's team, the impact is an average of a **31.6%** year-to-year growth in annual company revenue.

Leading marketers are realizing the treasure trove that is sales data and are beginning to use that data to inform their editorial calendars and creation cycles. Instead of content that only caters to the marketing funnel, smart marketers are now driving content that helps Sales and reduces friction points within the sales stage of the funnel.

Marketers everywhere need to create content that caters to the entire funnel to make it clear to Sales that Marketing is an essential part of the machine that increases company revenue. To do so, Marketing must learn to leverage their Sales team.

Make Marketing Decisions Based on Sales Data

Sales has a lot of data. Each salesperson tracks any or all of the following data points on a quarterly, monthly or weekly cycle:

- Win rates
- Number of deals closed
- Dollar amount of revenue generated
- Dollar amount in their pipeline
- Opportunities lost
- Competitors

That treasure trove of data is often housed within the Sales team. The data Sales has can give a marketer an incredible amount of clarity into what makes a customer buy, what makes them leave the funnel and what gets them stuck somewhere in the middle. If Sales is moving towards a more consultative approach, it's a marketer's job to arm them with the right content during every step.

Smart marketers need to keep a pulse on what's happening across their Sales team. Sharing sales data with the Marketing team is the first step into visibility.

I measure everything because I can't improve what I can't measure. So, it's all about recording what's working and not making decisions based on intuition, because the data never lies.

Eric Gonazlez
Senior Manager, Sales Development, Glassdoor

Join Forces and Build a Plan of Attack for Prospecting

Whether your organization has a dedicated prospecting team or your salespeople do their own prospecting, there are ways in which Marketing can enable the prospecting process.

In a study by LinkedIn titled "5 B2B Buyer Preferences to Know," it found that "nearly **90%** of B2B buyers are more likely to engage with sales professionals who are viewed as thought leaders in their industry." Thus, it's important that Marketing provides Sales with the right messaging, content and other collateral that will position them as thought leaders.

Our Sales and Marketing experts provided this comprehensive list of the types of collateral that Marketing can develop for your prospecting reps:

Create and curate content around why a topic (HR compliance, cloud storage, recruiting, etc.) matters to a prospect's specific role or industry.

 Buyer personas segment your audience and create stronger Sales and Marketing strategies.

 Ebooks are a strategic opportunity to present rich and engaging information to prospects.

 Case Studies demonstrate success while focusing on an individual customer's journey.

 Infographics visualize data points, statistics and best practices to salespeople in a direct visual way that requires minimal reading.

 Videos demonstrate instant value and are short yet effective enough to hold an attention span.

 Product Overview Sheet should be sent after a discovery call to quickly inform prospects on your solution.

 Call-to-action on your website where prospects have no other choice but to stop and take immediate action.

Help Sales Close Deals at the Final Stages with Content

Sales should never go into the pricing stage without an arsenal of Marketing collateral. At these final stages, the high-level collateral needs to shift towards elevating your products and why it justifies the cost.

Sales needs Marketing to achieve this. For aligned companies, this is where they generate hyper-specific content such as an in-depth blog articles, customer testimonials, interactive content and case studies.

> I think producing what Sales needs to close deals is the best use of Marketing's time. We make sure that our marketing lead generation is tightly tied to sales objectives, and we constantly check with Sales to make sure we're producing the volume of quality leads that will get them to quota.

Nick Christman
Marketing Director, Namely

Focus on the Entire Funnel

Marketing and Sales need to look at the entire sales funnel and integrate their forces to make the sales process more effective and content-driven. Both marketers and sales reps need to have their pulse on the entire sales funnel. Once you've got a pulse on the entire funnel, you can then build on that information and track the most powerful metrics, which we'll cover in the next chapter.

CHAPTER 3: METRICS THAT DRIVE ALIGNMENT

Sales and Marketing track a lot of metrics. In this chapter we'll breakdown all the soft metrics and tell you the three metrics that your organization can monitor to drive Sales and Marketing alignment.

Metric 1: Revenue per Lead

Revenue per lead is a unit metric that crosses between Sales and Marketing and tells you the efficiency of both your lead generation and sales closing efforts.

In measuring Revenue per lead, you need to take the amount of revenue generated and divide it by the number of leads generated during a pre-determined amount of time (example: a week or a month). For instance, if you generated leads during the first week of a quarter and the average closing rate for deals is 90 days, you can look at the revenue generated for that quarter and divide it by the number of leads.

This metric communicates to you not only how you're doing in generating revenue in comparison to costs of a lead, but it will also help you understand the productivity of a single salesperson.

This metric is also particularly valuable when you find out that you've doubled the number of leads generated month-over-month. With this metric, you can easily track whether the lift in leads is actually for quality, revenue-generating leads.

Metric 2: Conversion by Stage in Funnel

Instead of looking at separate funnels, both Sales and Marketing need to focus on one unified funnel and zero in on where opportunities are falling out.

The Conversion by stage in the funnel metric is ongoing and tracks the conversion rate within the sales funnel and pinpoints where Marketing can create content to prevent opportunities from leaving. In tracking this metric, both Sales and Marketing will be able to discern the friction points in the sales funnel. Typically, the sales funnel looks like this:

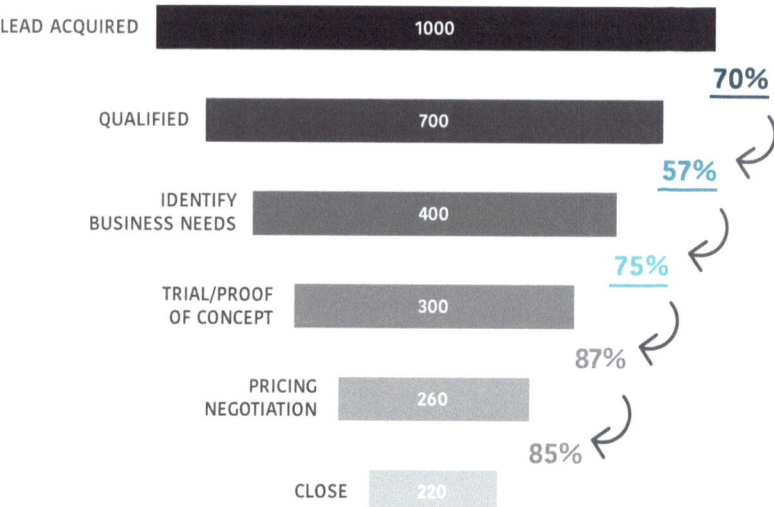

Once Sales and Marketing have figured out where opportunities are falling out of the funnel, both teams can collaborate to fix the leakage. If the historical data show that Sales struggles with converting an opportunity from qualified to identifying a prospect's business needs, this is where Sales and Marketing need to come together.

Marketing can create content that will drive the conversion percentage at this specific stage upward. Instead of guessing if

- the talk track is off,
- the marketing collateral created for this stage is thin,
- the competitive messaging and value proposition isn't strong enough,
- reps are not adequately armed enough to run through their demos.

Instead, let the data prove where to fix the problem.

> We're able to map the content out, and at each stage of the funnel, we actually have different pieces of content to move opportunities through the funnel, moving from awareness, consideration and closing.

My Truong
Direct Marketing Manager, Nexmo

Sales and Marketing need to focus their resources on the lowest performing conversion percentages because those are crucial points in the sales process and opportunities cannot fall out of the funnel.

For those of you that are focused on the post-sale side of the funnel, we've also seen incredible value being delivered through a collaboration between Marketing and Customer Success managers to move customers through their journey in using the process.

Metric 3: Usage of Marketing Collateral in the Sales Process

As we learned in metric two, Marketing must play a more significant role in the sales funnel. In Chapter Two, we discussed the types of collateral that Marketing must develop to drive awareness. Now, we're putting that collateral to use and getting critical feedback from Sales on its effectiveness.

On the next page, you'll find a worksheet that will help Sales give feedback to Marketing on collateral.

WORKSHEET
THE DEFINITIVE SCORING MATRIX FOR MARKETING COLLATERAL

	# of Times Used	Feedback Rating	# of Deals Closed with it	$ Value of the Deal	Stage Used in the Funnel
Product Overview					
Case Study					
Blog Article					
Talk Track by Stage in Funnel					
eBook					
Infographic					
Video					

COLLATERAL LEGEND:

PRODUCT OVERVIEW
Send your prospects a one page PDF about your product immediately after a call.

CASE STUDY
Showcase a customer's story on how your product helped solve their business needs.

BLOG ARTICLE
Send a hyper-relevant article that acts as a conversation starter with your prospects.

TALK TRACK BY STAGE IN FUNNEL
Plan to talk about all the relevant and pressing points for a prospect within any stage in the funnel.

EBOOK
Validate your expertise on a subject while sharing insights in a digestible format.

INFOGRAPHIC
Give your prospects useful information in a highly visual medium that gets the point across quickly.

VIDEO
Demonstrate an instant value in a short, yet effective medium that holds the busiest salesperson's attention span.

For the Scoring Matrix to be effective, Marketing needs to survey their Sales team for collateral feedback; if not Marketing runs the risk of missing out on valuable information.

- **Step 1**: Send out a brief digital survey with easy-to-answer, yet specific questions about the most recent piece of content.
- **Step 2**: Make sure Sales has enough time between content distribution and being able to actually use it in their sales process.
- **Step 3a**: If you're in Sales, be sure to use the content that Marketing has created.
- **Step 3b**: If you're in Marketing, be vocal about new content and know how to communicate to Sales.

> The Sales team is also my customer, so I need to figure out how to market to them and communicate with them. What I try to do is provide as much information as possible, and then once I find people who are early adopters, I elevate them and enable them to share their message and story about where they're finding success.

—
Christina House
Campaign Marketing, Tableau Software

Beyond Metrics

Metrics are an indicator of the health of your business. But, alignment is deeper than content, collaboration and metrics. Alignment is a core value. In the next chapter, you'll learn how you can integrate alignment as your company's core value.

CHAPTER 4: SALESPEOPLE ARE BECOMING MINI-MARKETERS

As Sales is moving towards being more customer-focused, sales reps must adopt new strategies that blend their Sales know-how with Marketing savviness. In a study by LinkedIn and IDC stated, "The fastest way to a B2B buyer's heart is through engaging their mind. B2B buyers are 5x more likely to engage with a sales professional who provides new insights about their business."

One of the fastest ways to engage a prospect's mind is to transform your Sales team into mini-marketers with four strategies:

Strategy #1: Teach Your Salespeople to Nurture the Top of the Funnel at Scale

The top of the funnel is the stage where salespeople must proactively engage with prospects to educate them on topics that concern their business. This is where the salespeople have the power to change a prospect's perspective and help them recognize their need for a new product. At this stage, salespeople should leverage content that will demonstrate expertise in their field.

This top level engagement will influence their conversion through the funnel. Nurturing at the top of the funnel can be executed at scale once you set the right tools in place. The 5x5 Method allows salespeople to stay top of mind for their prospects by sending out a pre-determined set of five emails over a length of time. During their campaign, salespeople need to rely on content because content plays a critical role throughout the tech-buying cycle. These emails should be to-the-point and written as valuable digestible nuggets of information.

INTRODUCE YOURSELF   PROVIDE VALUE   OFFER HELP   ENGAGE FOR FEEDBACK   "THE ASK"

Steps in the 5x5 Method

> At the top of the funnel, when a prospect isn't really engaged, we send out a lot of content such as eBooks and thought leadership. Then, later in the sales funnel, we send "How to Buy" guides and more focused content.

Eric Gonazlez
Senior Manager, Sales Development, Glassdoor

Sending out the campaign is step one; step two is monitoring its engagement rate to see which prospects are opening your emails, digesting the content and moving through the funnel.

Strategy #2: Build a Smart SDR Team

In traditional Sales organizations, reps did it all, from prospecting to closing deals. The modern Sales team is now segmented and hyper-specialized. According to the Selling Power Blog, "we need a disruptive approach to sales and customer engagement that allows sales reps to consistently perform as consultative, trusted advisors." That disruptive approach is building an incredibly agile and smart Sales Development team.

Sales Development Reps (SDR) Responsibilities

- Work the Top of the Funnel and proactively reach out to prospects
- Write hyper personalized email templates and emails at scale
- Create and monitor multi-touch email campaigns
- Build initial relationships with prospects
- Book meetings for Account Executives

SDRs use their strong analytical and research backgrounds in creative ways to start meaningful conversations with prospects. SDRs are a hungry and hard-working group of individuals that are eager to win, so arm them with the best thought leadership.

WORKSHEET
HIRING RUBRIC FOR YOUR SDR TEAM

- ☐ Bachelor's Degree or equivalent
- ☐ 6 - 12 months of phone experience
- ☐ High energy level, motivation and drive to succeed
- ☐ Proven track record of excellent communication
- ☐ Versatile enough to be a team player, but effective enough to be an individual contributor
- ☐ Strong passion for selling and ability to communicate a product's value
- ☐ Knowledge of Salesforce (a plus)

The SDR is a distinct strategic and competitive advantage for any ambitious sales team, so make it a key role for your organization.

Strategy #3: Have Your Salespeople Blog

Your sales reps are probably thinking that they don't have time to blog or it's not part of their job at your organization. Sales reps believe that they should spend all their time focused on prospecting, closing deals and updating Salesforce. Thus, they should spend zero time blogging. But, if a sales rep does choose to blog, they can reap the benefits just by publishing their first post.

Blogging isn't hard. Here's how your sales reps can approach blogging:

- Curate content and share (such as commenting on another blog article with their insight and adding an additional layer of sales expertise).
- Write about their own experiences and ideas (for more on how to get started, see the worksheet on the next page).

THE ULTIMATE BLOGGING 101 CHECKLIST FOR SALESPEOPLE

- ☐ Blog about what you know.

- ☐ Know your target audience (hint: it's your prospects).

- ☐ Get your ideas together.

- ☐ Form an opinion and take a stance.

- ☐ Start writing.

- ☐ Check for readability and ask yourself the following:

    - ☐ Is it scannable?

    - ☐ Does your headline grab attention?

    - ☐ Do you have a solid introduction?

    - ☐ Does your post flow smoothly from introduction to problem to solution?

    - ☐ Does it have a clear conclusion?

    - ☐ Does it have a call to action?

- ☐ Don't forget to publish and promote it.

You know a lot about the sales process, customer pain points and best practices, so blog about it. Say you came across an interesting article about Social Selling; you should provide commentary and give further insight into how social selling has helped you exceed your sales quota by **10%**.

" There's no quick path in becoming a thought leader. But, it all comes down to adding value. You are a thought leader when people see you as the ultimate resource around a specific topic. If people start coming to you, even if it's three or four people, then you're beginning to become a thought leader in the space. "

Koka Sexton
Group Manager, Content and Social Team, Corporate Communications, LinkedIn

Beyond thought leadership, each blog post that you write drives traffic to your company's website and it creates individual interest for you—as a salesperson and a thought leader. Every time you write a blog post, it gets indexed on your company's website and drives more Google search results for your company and yourself.

Every time you hit publish, you're not just posting to your company's blog, you're sharing your expertise and insights to a combined audience of Twitter, Facebook, LinkedIn and Google+, which can expose your voice to an exponential audience.

THE POWER OF BLOGGING

434%+
COMPANIES THAT BLOG HAVE
434% MORE INDEXED PAGES
AND GET **MORE LEADS.**

67%
B2B MARKETERS WHO USE BLOGS
GENERATE **67% MORE** LEADS
THAN THOSE THAT DO NOT.

*Source: SEO Power Suite, Yahoo!

81%

OF BUSINESSES CONSIDER THEIR BLOGS TO BE AN **IMPORTANT ASSET** TO THEIR BUSINESS.

37%

OF MARKETERS SAY BLOGS ARE **THE MOST VALUABLE TYPE** OF CONTENT MARKETING.

60%

OF CONSUMERS FEEL **MORE POSITIVE** ABOUT A COMPANY AFTER READING CUSTOM CONTENT ON ITS SITE.

 Make sure each blog post has your picture, a short bio and contact information, so prospects can easily reach out to you.

See example below:

About Dan Smith

Dan Smith is a Sales Happiness Officer at ToutApp. He once almost did CPR on Michael Jackson.

Start blogging, because one hour of effort can lead to exponential views and future leads, and it can grow your career as a thought leader.

Strategy #4: Collaborate with Marketing & Form a Line of Communication

Armed with the three strategies discussed in this chapter, it's important to emphasize that to make this all possible, you need to collaborate and communicate with Marketing.

We cannot stress how important collaboration and open communication is to driving Sales and Marketing alignment. Without communication, it would be impossible to talk about content, gain insight into each other's teams and track the metrics that matter. It's too often that Sales and Marketing teams work in separate offices, with different tools, misaligned goals and no clear line of communication. That cannot happen anymore.

Sales Reps and Marketers Take Note

Today, the blog is the starting place for online content. In fact, according to the blog Social Media Today, **70%** of consumers learn about a company through articles rather than ads. So, empower your salespeople to become mini-marketers through nurturing the top of the funnel at scale, sales development reps, blogging and collaborating with Marketing.

CHAPTER 5: ATTENTION MARKETING: DON'T SEND SALES EMAILS ON BEHALF OF SALES

O ften times, Marketing will send emails on behalf of Sales. And that's a disservice to the sales process. No one wants a marketing email that's disguised as a sales email.

Marketing emails are designed to look attractive and promote your product, an upcoming event, popular posts on the company blog, etc. Marketing emails package information and wrap a bow around it with little to no personalization within the body of the email itself.

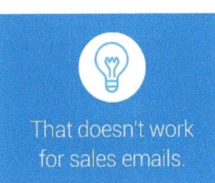
That doesn't work for sales emails.

However in marketing automation, Marketing will send emails to support the Sales process. Those emails, whether a salesperson is sending them or Marketing is sending them, must look and feel like real emails. That's important because Marketing emails should look like they're sent from marketing while, sales emails should look like emails sent by a human.

Send a Real Email

Sales is about building authentic relationships with prospects that rely on the exchange of knowledge and concerns. Sales reps need to show that they're human and not sales bot. First step: make sure you're sending emails from your email address.

None of this **sales@domain.com** and more of this **anna@domain.com**.

Sending a real email, from a real email address, automatically gives your email a personal touch and sets the tone for the rest of your email.

Offer Valuable Information

Today, **65%** of all email gets opened on a mobile device. To cut through the inbox noise, you have to make a great first impression, and that starts with your subject line. Your subject line must offer something valuable right away.

 Don't forget to **A/B test** your email **subject lines**. There are tools (read: **ToutApp**) that will help you uncover the best performing subject lines.

Then, you need to build on that momentum and continue to offer valuable information that keeps prospects motivated to read the actual email. How do you do this? You hyper-personalize your email by sprinkling it with the following

- a {{Hi First_Name}}
- a commonality that you have with them (so take your time and do research)
- a genuine interest in them

Then immediately get to the point and address their concerns or give them a unique industry perspective.

Keep It Simple

In building on what we've learned above about offering valuable information, to take your emails to the next level, you have to keep them simple. Don't overcomplicate it with too much jargon, too much text or too many links.

Often times, marketing emails are too broad, have too many ideas going on at once and confuse the reader. Instead, keep your emails focused on one topic with one blog article, research study or other hyper-relevant links. Why? Because it makes it easier on your prospects and it drives attention to your overall message.

Have One Call to Action

The point of any sales email is to offer a unique benefit, whether it's a new way to look at a prospect's industry or the trial of a new product. Keep your sales email to a singular call to action. You need to explicitly tell your prospect at the end of the email what their next steps are if they're interested.

Partner with Marketing

It's not to say that Sales and Marketing can't work together to create great sales emails. In fact, Sales and Marketing should work together on email templates that focus on the right messaging to connect with prospects.

> Marketing can do the adverse thing and turn people off in terms of their marketing drip campaigns, even if they don't intend to do so. But, if I get an email from a real person and it's a tailored email, I'm more likely to remember them and move along the funnel.

Kyle Poretto
Former Sales Development Manager, NewsCred

Having Marketing send your sales emails isn't authentic. Often times, they can do more harm than help in the situation. But when Sales and Marketing collaborate, they can start effective conversations through emails.

Translating what works for Marketing into Sales strategy isn't the answer. But, taking elements from Marketing might be the silver bullet.

CHAPTER 6: HOW TO PULL IT ALL TOGETHER

I n the past five chapters, you've collaborated on creating content, analyzed data, tracked the right metrics and learned how to write great blog posts. Now, here's how you put all of that learned information together and truly bring alignment to your organization. Remember, **80%** (unless we fix that statistic) of the content created won't get used, so this last mile is important.

Here are the final three steps that drive alignment between Sales and Marketing:

Step #1: Package Content for Easy Access for Sales

Salespeople don't have time to find content; they're focused on writing emails and closing deals. Marketers are frustrated because they don't have insight into which pieces of content Sales is using and if they are focused on the right messaging.

 Marketers need to package up content as an email template to empower Sales to use it.

 Use the Scoring Matrix for Marketing Collateral found in Chapter Three to get feedback and usage data.

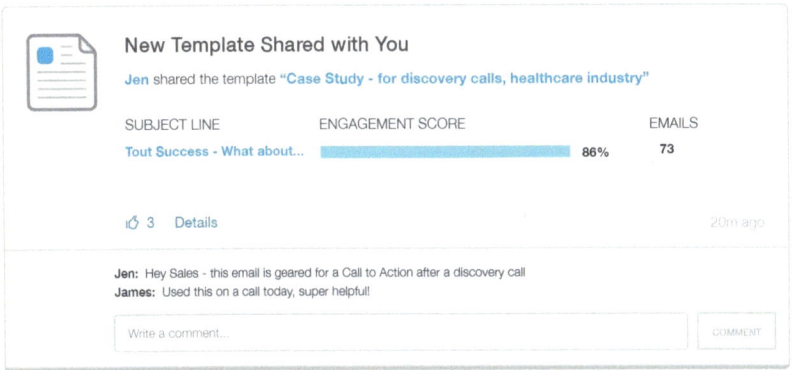

New Template Shared with You

Jen shared the template "Case Study - for discovery calls, healthcare industry"

SUBJECT LINE	ENGAGEMENT SCORE		EMAILS
Tout Success - What about...		86%	73

👍 3   Details   20m ago

Jen: Hey Sales - this email is geared for a Call to Action after a discovery call
James: Used this on a call today, super helpful!

Write a comment...   COMMENT

Engagement Data via ToutApp's Sales Beat

Marketers need to keep a pulse on what's happening on the sales floor. If a prospect requires multiple touches of nurturing during their sales process, Marketing needs to arm Sales with the right content (more on types of content in *Chapters One* and *Three*) to educate prospects. Having an arsenal of case studies, product one pagers and industry research studies packaged into an email template is indispensable.

Sales needs to have access to consistent messaging and data-proven engaging content right when they need it. And Marketing needs real-time insights into what types of content Sales is using. Thus, it's incredibly important for Marketing to package content into emails that empower Sales to use them during their sales process.

Step #2: Contextualize and Track Email Templates

If Sales and Marketing truly want alignment, Marketing cannot just write an email template, send it to Sales and simply walk away. Marketing needs to put context around their content and email templates, so their content doesn't end up adding to the **80%** statistic. This additional layer of context is the key that empowers Sales to use Marketing-generated content. Contextualization is a must if Sales wants to deliver powerful messages to their prospects, and this contextualization must come from Marketing.

Before sending out a packaged email template to Sales, Marketing needs to contextualize the email and say that this email template is for this stage in the sales funnel for this industry, role, etc. Today's buyer is smarter, has more information available to him or her and has less time for nonsense. Contextualizing emails for Sales eliminates those roadblocks. On the next page, learn how Marketing can thoroughly package content for sales usage and provide context around content and use cases.

HOW MARKETING CAN THOROUGHLY PACKAGE CONTENT FOR SALES USAGE

☐ **Step 1**: Get a piece of content.

    ☐ If you have a piece of content that's dynamic and useful that conveys a great story, write a template for it.

☐ **Step 2**: During your meeting with Sales, discuss where this specific piece of content will be most valuable during their sales funnel.

    ☐ Listen to the feedback.

    ☐ What should you change?

    ☐ What questions were asked, and how could you better prepare?

☐ **Step 3**: Write a concise email template for Sales.
Is the subject line positive?

    ☐ Does the body of the email grab the reader's attention?

    ☐ Remember to attach or link to the piece of content.

☐ **Step 4**: Share the email template with Sales.

    ☐ Give them specific use cases.

    ☐ Share the email template and notify Sales on multiple channels (group chat, email, company meetings, collaboration tools, etc.).

☐ **Step 5**: Monitor usage.

    ☐ Get feedback and iterate.

After every step is checked off, only then can Sales take immediate action and deploy those emails to their prospects.

Step #3: Track and Measure Usage

Then, Marketing needs to track and measure the usage and engagement data attached to each email and discern its success rate (which depends on how success is defined at your organization: views, clicks, sign-ups, calls, etc). Additionally, Sales and Marketing can A/B test templates side by side to see which template is higher performing.

This engagement data then becomes a shared metric. Both teams will know what works, how the numbers prove that it works, how many deals were closed by using this specific email template and the timeframe it took to close a deal.

Conclusion

Taking what we've learned in the previous chapters of this book, Marketing will get a better understanding of the sales process and will know how to concentrate their resources in building a refined and robust content library for each stage in the sales funnel. For Sales, they'll have to resources they need to have a more streamlined and hyper-focused sales process and are overall better equipped to do their job.

When Sales is armed with the right content, data, statistics and actionable steps that are provided by Marketing, only then will your organization achieve alignment. After all, statistics show that aligned organizations experience an average of **31.6%** revenue growth year-over-year. So, if you want alignment, take action now.

 Collaboration isn't something you implement, check the box and say you're done. It starts as soon as you have Sales and Marketing, evolves with your business, and dies if you don't continue to reinvest in it. At Namely, we sit together and keep a constant dialogue going on how we grow revenue together.

Nick Christman
Marketing Director, Namely

Alignment has to start from the top down and there has to be alignment on the objectives for Sales and objectives for Marketing. Then we agree on priorities and what we're trying to achieve within the organization. We have to have alignment down to the minute details.

Tejal Parekh
VP of Marketing

SALES & MARKETING ALIGNMENT SUCCESS STORY: HACKERRANK

Building Out An Aligned Organization

When Alison Boehler joined HackerRank in late 2013, the company didn't have a Marketing team. If Alison wanted a sales deck, a solution brief or any type of marketing collateral, it was up to her to create it. In 2014, Tejal Parekh joined as the VP of Marketing and began to build out a Marketing team that works in collaboration with Sales.

As Tejal helped grow the team, she hired marketers who have a mastery in Marketing, but also have a firm understanding of Sales. On the Sales side, HackerRank coincidentaly hired salespeople with Marketing experience. This two-way understanding of each other's roles has helped tremendously in communication and collaboration across Sales and Marketing.

The Key to Alignment

"I think there are two things: transparency and accountability. Transparency is a form of being absolutely clear on goals, commitments and expectations. Every quarter, that process needs to be addressed. And once you've agreed on certain objectives, then it's about accountability. If you're agreeing on what your team is going to deliver, you have to follow through on those commitments."

Tejal Parekh
VP of Marketing

HackerRank

HackerRank is a platform that helps programmers develop their skills and companies recruit top-notch tech talent. The platform is open to anyone, with a focus on those who want to hone their tech skills in any computer science domain. The company has been able to scale their product and drive rapid growth through true alignment between Sales and Marketing.

Industry:
Computer Software

Company Size:
51 - 200 employees

Location:
Mountain View, CA

Constant communication helps drive successful alignment. At HackerRank, we found that when Sales and Marketing take on ventures together, such as a monthly webinar, we're more successful.

Alison Boehler
Sales Effectiveness Leader

For HackerRank, Sales and Marketing alignment is a core value and is about building trust with one another. Without accountability or without follow-through, companies run the risk of losing trust and it will inadvertently affect their bottom line revenue.

Actionable Sales and Marketing Alignment

At HackerRank, the company hosts a monthly webinar where Sales and Marketing can put their alignment into action.

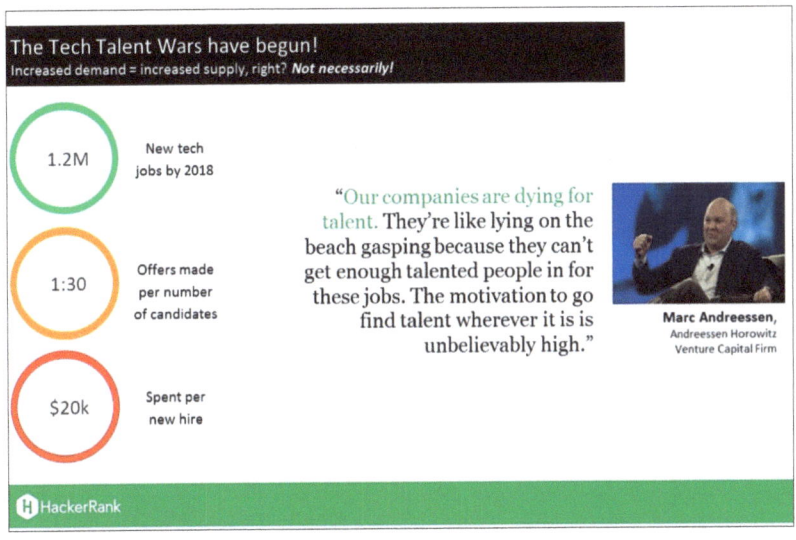

HackerRank Webinar: How to Hire Tech Talent
Through Skill Not School (2015)

TOOLS FOR SALES & MARKETING ALIGNMENT

TOUTAPP

Tracking
Never send a blind email again. For both Sales and Marketing, know exactly when a prospect, customer or colleague opens your email.

Templates
Successful organizations rely on templates to save time and send out the right messaging. Marketing can write templates for Sales, and Sales can deploy each on-brand template in every sales scenario.

Analytics
Rely on Tout Analytics to inform both your Sales and Marketing teams on the data and emails that work and what doesn't work.

Sales Beat
With Sales Beat, your teams can get real-time insights to get every deal done to work smarter, together.

CLOUD STORAGE / LIBRARY

Sales and Marketing will be able to learn about what the other team is working on and how to position themselves to prospects and customers.

Organization is key in aligning Sales and Marketing. You must have a central hub for all content, including case studies, infographics and videos.

GROUP CHAT

Sales and Marketing need a tool where they can talk to each other in real-time and all in one place.

CONTENT MANAGEMENT SYSTEM

Whether you choose WordPress, LinkedIn Pulse or Medium as platforms for content, you have to have a central system for it.

SALES & MARKETING EXPERTS

Alison Boehler
Sales Effectiveness Leader, HackerRank / @AlisonBoehler

HackerRank is a platform that helps developers expand their skills and companies recruit top tech talent.
Industry: Computer Software
Company Size: 51- 200 employees
Location: Mountain View, CA

Tomasz Borys
Director of Marketing, KISSmetrics / @tbcali

KISSmetrics provides web analytics solutions to assist companies in customer acquisition and decision-making.
Industry: Internet
Company Size: 51- 200 employees
Location: San Francisco, CA

Nick Christman
Marketing Director, Namely / @nickxman

Namely is a leading HR and payroll platform for scaling companies and is used by some of the world's most innovative companies.
Industry: Computer Software
Company Size: 51- 200 employees
Location: New York, NY

Eric Gonzalez
Senior Manager, Sales Development, Glassdoor / @EricGonz

Glassdoor is the most transparent jobs and career marketplace and is changing how people search for jobs and how companies recruit candidates.
Industry: Internet
Company Size: 201- 500 employees
Location: Mill Valley, CA

Christina House
Campaign Manager, Tableau Software

Tableau makes it easy for people to rapidly transform data into smart business analytics and simplifies the way data is explored and communicated.
Industry: Computer Software
Company Size: 1001- 5000 employees
Location: Seattle, WA

Tejal Parekh
VP of Marketing, HackerRank / @TejalParekh

HackerRank is a platform that helps developers expand their skills and companies recruit top tech talent.
Industry: Computer Software
Company Size: 51- 200 employees
Location: Mountain View, CA

Kyle Poretto
Former SDR Manager, NewsCred / @kyleporetto

NewsCred is the leading content marketing platform that is powering marketing technology for the future and helping brands transform how they connect with people.
Industry: Marketing and Advertising
Company Size: 201- 500 employees
Location: New York, NY

Koka Sexton
Group Manager, Content and Social Team, Corporate Communications, LinkedIn / @kokasexton

LinkedIn connects the world's professionals to make them more productive and successful and is the largest professional network on the Internet.
Industry: Internet
Company Size: 5001- 10000 employees
Location: Mountain View, CA

My Truong
Direct Marketing Manager, Nexmo / @PtitMy

Nexmo provides innovative cloud communication APIs that enable applications and enterprises to connect with their customers through phone and SMS.
Industry: Computer Software
Company Size: 51- 200 employees
Location: San Francisco, CA

Before Tout, we sent blind emails and hoped they were opened. Now, we have full visibility to actively manage the 2,500 leads in our funnel at any given time.

Jonathan Bolger
Senior Account Executive at MINDBODY

TOUTAPP IS BUILT TO
EMPOWER SALESPEOPLE

ToutApp helps salespeople close more deals with the power of Tracking, Templates and Analytics, plugged directly into Gmail, Outlook and Salesforce.

SALES REPS
Close deals faster with integrated sales intelligence and productivity tools

Close more deals with complete visibility across the sales cycle

SALES MANAGERS
Streamline your sales process and increase rep productivity

Increase productivity while maintaining the personal touch with your prospects

MARKETING
Arm your Sales team with the best content and email templates

Measure and improve messaging using real-time data that tells you what works

THE MOST **INNOVATIVE SALES TEAMS** USE TOUT

Namely

REFERENCES

Aberdeen Group. Sales and Marketing Alignment. N.p.: n.p., n.d. PDF.

Butler, Bill. "Give Your Sales Team a New Game Plan for Engaging Customers."
Selling Power Blog. N.p., 22 Apr. 2015. Web.

Content Marketing Institute, and MarketingProfs. B2B Content Marketing 2015
Benchmarks, Budgets, and Trends - North America. N.p.: Content Marketing
Institute, 2015. PDF.

Fidelman, Mark. "Study: 78% Of Salespeople Using Social Media Outsell Their
Peers." Forbes. Forbes Magazine, 19 Mar. 2013. Web. 2015.

Garibian, Lenna. "Content Plays Critical Role Throughout Tech-Buying Cycle."
MarketingProfs. N.p., 23 Oct. 2012. Web. 2015.

"IDC Home: The Premier Global Market Intelligence Firm." www.idc.com. N.p.,
n.d. Web. May 2015.

LinkedIn, and IDC. "5 B2B Buyer Preferences to Know." 5 B2B Buyer Preferences
to Know. N.p., 24 Sept. 2014. Web. 2015.

Liubarets, Tatiana. "Top Blogging Statistics: 45 Reasons to Blog." Yahoo Small
Business. N.p., n.d. Web. 2015.

McGrail, Mike. "The Blogconomy: Blogging Stats [INFOGRAPHIC]." Social Media
Today. N.p., 28 Aug. 2013. Web. 2015.

Siu, Eric. "24 Eye-Popping SEO Statistics - Search Engine Journal." Search
Engine Journal. N.p., 19 Apr. 2012. Web. 2015.

"What Are the Benefits of Sales & Marketing Alignment? I2 20% Growth
Enough?" Selling Power Blog. N.p., 19 Oct. 2010. Web. 2015.